Acknowledgements

Empowerment Prayers (Kids) is a vision that started on Whatsapp. I sent out prayers to two praise and worship leaders which evolved into my whole contact list. It has now taken on a life of it's own on social media and Empowerment Prayers reaches many people from our blogs to the many pages on Facebook, Instagram and Twitter with prayers and words of encouragement. This vision is bigger than social media and I did not just want to empower adults alone, I wanted to reach children too! Today that vision has been realised with the launch of our book, Empowerment Prayers (Kids), an illustrated prayer book for children.

With that being said, I want to express my sincere and special thanks to the Lord Jesus Christ for seeing me through and giving me the grace to continue with this vision to the end, even when I wanted to stop because I felt the vision was too big. You have truly kept me, and put some great people around me that have helped me in a tremendous way.

To those special people along the way, thank you ever so much. To my mum, and mummaja, Portia Joseph, thank you for believing in me and pushing me to do this until it was completed.

Thanks to my grandmother, Enid Joseph, and sister, Lauren Derby, thank you too, for always being there and encouraging me when it was hard to carry on. To my Godmother, Mable Hall, thank you for taking the time to help me along the way. To Shean Roberts, thank you for the endless get-togethers, and the continuous help you give to me.

To my mentor, Andrea Johnson, thank you for your investment in me, your time and great leadership that you continually bestow on me, and always reminding me of what I can achieve if I believe in myself. Thank you all so much, I appreciate you all and love you all very much.

Chloe

GREENShoot

PUBLISHING

Content

Morning Time Prayer

Beloved Father, thank you for this day yo
have made and for waking me up to see thi
new day. To have eyes to see, ears to hea
and movement in my body.

I pray today shall be a great day with ever
step I take and every move I make, in you
name Jesus,

Amen

Night Time Prayer

Beloved Father, in Heaven as I lay my hea
to sleep, watch over me and keep me safe a
I am sleeping.

Keep me safe through the night and be wit
me at all times; let no harm come near thi
bed and let your peace remain in this plac
in Jesus name I pray,

Amen

Grace (blessing your food) Prayer

Thank you for the food I am about to receive Father; bless every hand that made it and I thank you for providing me with something to eat.

Bless this food as I receive it now in Jesus name,

Amen

Forgiveness Prayer

Beloved Father, I ask for your help that I will be able to forgive those that have hurt me and have not said nice things about me or make me cry.

I know that I should forgive because you forgive me when I do something wrong, so help me Jesus to be more like you and not be quick to get upset.

Let me love in the way you do in Jesus name I pray,

Amen

13

To Hear God's Voice Prayer

Father, help me to know your voice more each day as I get to know you in speaking with you through prayer and everyday life.

Help me to pay attention to the small still soft voice inside of me with my listening ears turned on to do right from wrong.

That I shall never fear, but from within be bold, brave and courageous, doing all that you say because I know it is for my good, in Jesus name I pray,

Amen

15

Thanksgiving (Thankful) Prayer

Father God, I just want to take this time out to say thank you for all I have in my life. For having family, parents, my siblings, my house and even this beautiful world that you have made and given us Lord Jesus.

Thank you for everything, even the things and people I may have even left out of this prayer.

I am thankful for it all Jesus and I give you all the honour and praise; with a heart full of thanksgiving in Jesus name I pray,

Amen

17

An Apologetic (Sorry) Prayer

Beloved Father, sorry for the things I may have done, the way I treated people today and the things that may have caused somebody hurt in any way, shape or form. I am truly sorry for the way I acted and behaved.

Thank you Father that you are a loving God and you hear my prayer of saying sorry.

May tomorrow be a better day in Jesus name I pray,

Amen

19

Love Prayer

Beloved Father, in the Holy Bible it says you are loving, you are caring, you are patient and kind and much more Lord.

I ask you Father God to help me be like you in all my ways, that everywhere I go my family, friends, people known and unknown to me see God through me and that His love in me will shine bright to those near and far

Help me beloved Father burst through with love in every part of my life in Jesus name I pray,

Amen

21

Exam/Test Prayer

Beloved Father in Heaven, today I have a test; I ask for your help to remember all the information that I need and that I do not forget anything.

Father be with my hands as I write the words and sentences down. Also help me to remain calm, collected, focused and not nervous. I know with you all things are possible and that you oh Lord will be right beside me during the test.

I thank you in advance for all the success given to me in this exam/test this day in Jesus name I pray,

Amen

23

Purpose Prayer

Beloved Father in heaven, the Holy Bible says "You know the plans you have for my life, to give me a future and a hope; for good in my life and not evil."

Lord Jesus help me to be all that you have called me to be. With every move I make and every step I take guide and lead my feet down the right path. I pray to fulfill that which you have purposed me to do.

I pray that no matter how hard something is that I shall continue to the end never giving up because you are intentional about me and you want the best for me in Jesus name I pray,

Amen

24

25

Morning Prayer
(Write your own prayer here)

Night Time Prayer
(Write your own prayer here)

Grace (blessing your food) Prayer
(Write your own prayer here)

Forgiveness Prayer
(Write your own prayer here)

Thanksgiving (Thankful) Prayer
(Write your own prayer here)

An apologetic (sorry) prayer
(Write your own prayer here)

Exam/Test Prayer
(Write your own prayer here)

Love Prayer

(Write your own prayer here)

33